Party Food

Everyday recipes to enjoy

Bath · New York · Singapore · Hong Kong · Cologne · Delhi
Melbourne · Amsterdam · Johannesburg · Shenzhen

hummus

ingredients

SERVES 6

225 g/8 oz canned chickpeas, drained

150 ml/5 fl oz tahini, well stirred

150 ml/5 fl oz olive oil, plus extra to serve

2 garlic cloves, coarsely chopped

6 tbsp lemon juice

1 tbsp chopped fresh mint

salt and pepper

1 tsp paprika

Pitta bread, to serve

method

1 Put the chickpeas, tahini, olive oil and 150 ml/5 fl oz water into the blender and process briefly. Add the garlic, lemon juice and mint and process until smooth.

2 Check the consistency of the hummus and, if it is too thick, add 1 tablespoon water and process again. Continue adding water, 1 tablespoon at a time, until the right consistency is achieved. Hummus should have a thick, coating consistency. Season with salt and pepper to taste.

3 Spoon the hummus into a serving dish. Make a shallow hollow in the top and drizzle with 2–3 tablespoons olive oil. Cover with clingfilm and chill until required. Dust lightly with paprika and serve with pitta bread.

aubergine & pepper dip

ingredients

SERVES 6–8

2 large aubergines

2 red peppers

4 tbsp olive oil

2 garlic cloves, roughly
  chopped

grated rind and juice of
  $1/2$ lemon

1 tbsp chopped fresh
  coriander

$1/2$–1 tsp paprika

pepper

bread or toast, to serve

method

1 Preheat the oven to 190ºC/375ºF/Gas Mark 5. Prick the skins of the aubergines and peppers all over with a fork and brush with about 1 tablespoon of the olive oil. Put on a baking tray and bake in the oven for 45 minutes, or until the skins are beginning to turn black, the flesh of the aubergine is very soft and the peppers are deflated.

2 When the vegetables are cooked, put them in a bowl and immediately cover tightly with a clean, damp tea towel. Alternatively, you can put the vegetables in a plastic bag. Leave them for about 15 minutes until they are cool enough to handle.

3 When the vegetables have cooled, cut the aubergines in half lengthways, carefully scoop out the flesh and discard the skin. Cut the aubergine flesh into large chunks. Remove and discard the stem, core and seeds from the peppers and cut the flesh into large pieces.

4 Heat the remaining olive oil in a large, heavy-based frying pan, add the aubergine flesh and pepper pieces and fry for 5 minutes. Add the garlic and fry for a further 30 seconds.

5 Turn all the contents of the frying pan onto kitchen paper to drain, then transfer to the bowl of a food processor. Add the lemon rind and juice, the chopped coriander, the paprika, and pepper to taste, and blend until a rough purée is formed.

6 Place the dip in a serving bowl accompanied by slices of bread or toast.

salted almonds

ingredients

SERVES 6

4 tbsp olive oil

225 g/8 oz whole almonds,
    blanched

coarse sea salt

1 tsp paprika or ground
    cumin (optional)

method

1 Preheat the oven to 180°C/350°F/Gas Mark 4. Place the olive oil in a roasting tin and swirl it around so that it covers the base. Add the almonds and toss them in the tin so that they are evenly coated in the oil, then spread them out in a single layer.

2 Roast the almonds in the preheated oven for 20 minutes, or until they are light golden brown, tossing several times during the cooking. Drain the almonds on kitchen paper, then transfer them to a bowl.

3 While the almonds are still warm, sprinkle with plenty of sea salt and paprika or cumin, if using, and toss together to coat. Serve the almonds warm or cold. The almonds are at their best when served freshly cooked, so, if possible, cook them on the day that you plan to eat them. However, they can be stored in an airtight container for up to 3 days.

mini tartlets with scallops and pea & mint purée

ingredients

SERVES 12

100 g/3½ oz puff pastry rolled
    to a depth of 3mm/⅛ inch
4 large fresh scallops, cleaned
    and roe removed
salt and pepper
  extra virgin olive oil for coating
    the scallops

pea & mint purée

50 g/2 oz cooked peas
1 small garlic clove, grated
1 tbsp extra virgin olive oil
1 tbsp chopped mint
1 tbsp soured cream
1 tsp lemon juice
salt and pepper

method

1 Preheat the oven to 180°C/ 350°F/Gas Mark 4. Using a 4-cm/1½-inch round pastry cutter, cut out 12 pastry discs. Re-roll and use the puff pastry leftovers if there is not enough to make 12 discs.

2 Place the pastry discs on a flat tray, lined with greaseproof paper. Lay another layer of greaseproof paper over the top and then place a slightly smaller flat tray on top. (This will prevent the puff pastry from rising in the oven.)

3 Leave the pastry to rest for 20 minutes in a cool place before baking in the oven for 15–20 minutes or until golden. Remove and leave to cool.

4 To make the pea and mint purée, blend the peas in a food processor and add the garlic, extra virgin olive oil, mint, soured cream, lemon juice, and salt and pepper to taste. Process until combined. Scrape the mixture into a small container and place in the refrigerator.

5 Heat a non-stick frying pan until just smoking. Toss the scallops in a little extra virgin olive oil and season with salt and pepper to taste. Add the scallops to the pan and cook for 30 seconds each side. Remove the scallops from the pan and set aside.

6 To assemble the canapés, place a small amount of pea and mint purée on each mini tartlet. Cut each scallop into three slices and arrange on top of the canapés. Serve immediately on scallop shells, if liked.

crostini canapès

ingredients

MAKES 20

1 thin French baguette, sliced

extra-virgin olive oil

gorgonzola cheese with caramelized onions

2 large red onions, thinly
    sliced

25 g/1 oz butter

40 g/1½ oz caster sugar

225 ml/8 fl oz water

about 175 g/6 oz gorgonzola
    cheese

tomato, avocado & bacon

55 g/2 oz bacon, chopped

1 tbsp olive oil, plus extra
    if needed

1 large tomato, cored, seeded
    and finely diced

1–2 tbsp lemon juice, plus
    extra if needed

1–2 tbsp extra-virgin olive oil

2 tbsp finely shredded basil
    leaves

pinch of sugar

salt and pepper

1 avocado

method

1 Pre-heat the grill and place the bread slices on the grill rack about 10 cm/4 inches from the source of the heat. Toast slowly for 6–8 minutes, turning once, until crisp and golden on both sides. Leave to cool.

2 To make the caramelized onions, put the onions, butter and half the sugar in a saucepan with the water and bring to the boil. Reduce the heat and simmer, uncovered, for about 20 minutes until the onions are tender and the water has evaporated. Transfer the onions to a frying pan, sprinkle with the remaining sugar and stir over medium-high heat until the sugar melts and the onions are a light golden brown.

3 To make the tomato, avocado and bacon topping, put the chopped bacon and olive oil in a frying pan over medium-high heat and stir for about 5 minutes until the bacon is crisp. Remove from the pan, drain on kitchen paper and then transfer to a bowl. Add the tomato dice, lemon juice, olive oil, basil, sugar and salt and pepper to taste and stir. Cut the avocado in half, remove the stone and peel, then finely dice the flesh. Add to the bowl and gently stir together, making sure the avocado is well coated so it doesn't turn brown; add extra lemon juice or olive oil, if necessary.

4 When ready to serve, cover 12 crostini with a small slice of gorgonzola cheese, then top with a dollop of the caramalized onions. Top the remaining crostini with the tomato, avocado and bacon mixture. Alternatively, serve the crostini in a large, napkin-lined basket and offer the toppings in separate bowls. Let guests help themselves – be sure to have a couple of teaspoons on saucers beside the bowls of toppings.

cheese fondue with crudités

ingredients

SERVES 12

1 garlic clove, halved

225 g/8 oz Gruyère cheese, grated

1 tbsp plain flour

250 ml/9 fl oz dry or medium white wine

pinch of nutmeg

to serve

bread, cut into chunks

cooked sausages

cubed apple or pear

method

1 Rub the inside of a non-metallic fondue pot with the cut garlic and set aside. Mix the grated cheese and flour together thoroughly in a bowl.

2 Heat the wine in a saucepan over a medium heat. Gradually add the cheese mixture, 1 tablespoon at a time, stirring constantly in a zigzag motion with a wooden spoon. This will prevent the cheese from forming lumps as it cooks. Add the nutmeg and bring the mixture to a simmer, without boiling.

3 Transfer the mixture to the fondue pot and keep warm over the flame of the burner. Serve immediately with a selection of bread, sausages and cubes of apple or pear, for dipping.

mezze to share

ingredients

SERVES 2

quick hummus

400 g/14 oz canned chickpeas

2 garlic cloves, crushed

1 tbsp tahini paste

1 tbsp lemon juice, plus extra
    to taste

$1/4$ tsp ground cumin

3 tbsp extra virgin olive oil,
    plus extra for drizzling

paprika, for dusting

warm pitta bread, to serve

grilled halloumi cheese

225 g/8 oz halloumi cheese,
    sliced

olive oil, for brushing

juice of $1/2$ lemon

1 tsp chopped fresh oregano
    or mint, to garnish

chilli garlic prawns

140 g/5 oz cooked, peeled
    prawns

1 garlic clove, finely chopped

$1/4$ tsp hot chilli sauce

25 g/1 oz butter

method

1 To make the hummus, drain the chickpeas reserving the liquid. Put the chickpeas, garlic, tahini paste, lemon juice, cumin and olive oil in a blender or food processor. Process until almost smooth, adding a little of the reserved liquid if the mixture is very thick. Taste and add more lemon juice if needed. Spoon into a bowl and chill until required. Serve drizzled with a little olive oil, a dusting of paprika and the warm pitta bread on the side.

2 To prepare the halloumi cheese, brush each halloumi slice on both sides with a little olive oil. Heat a large non-stick frying pan and cook the cheese for 1 minute on each side, or until golden. Transfer the cheese to a warm plate and squeeze the lemon juice over the top. Sprinkle with chopped oregano or mint and serve immediately.

3 To make the chilli garlic prawns, mix together the prawns, garlic and chilli sauce in a bowl. Melt the butter in a pan and add the prawn mixture. Cook for 2 minutes, or until heated through. Serve immediately.

pretty chicory bites

ingredients

SERVES 8

3 medium-sized heads chicory

125 g/4^{1}/$_{2}$ oz blue cheese,
    such as Stilton, finely
    crumbled

4 tbsp pecan halves, very
    finely chopped

1 punnet mustard cress,
    to garnish

dressing

100 ml/3^{1}/$_{2}$ fl oz extra-virgin
    olive oil

2^{1}/$_{2}$ tbsp balsamic vinegar

1 tsp Dijon mustard

1 tsp sugar

salt and pepper

method

1 To make the dressing, put the oil, vinegar, mustard, sugar and salt and pepper to taste in a screw-top jar and shake until blended. Taste and adjust the seasoning, then set aside until required. (The prepared dressing can be stored in the refrigerator for up to three days.)

2 Cut the bases off the chicory heads so you can separate the leaves. Pick over the leaves and select the 24 best, boat-shaped leaves, then rinse them and pat dry.

3 Put the cheese and pecans in a bowl and gently toss together. Add 2 tablespoons of the dressing and toss again.

4 Arrange the chicory leaves on serving platters, then put a teaspoon of the cheese and pecans towards the pointed end of each leaf. Garnish each leaf with a few pieces of mustard cress. Cover and chill for up to an hour before serving.

spinach, feta & tomato triangles

ingredients

MAKES 12

2 tbsp olive oil

2 tbsp finely chopped shallot

115 g/4 oz fresh spinach,
    washed and shredded

2 sheets filo pastry

115 g/4 oz feta cheese,
    crumbled

6 sun-dried tomatoes,
    chopped finely

115 g/4 oz butter, melted

salt and pepper

method

1 Preheat the oven to 200°C/400°F/Gas Mark 6. Heat the oil in a pan over a medium heat and cook the shallot for 2–3 minutes. Add the spinach, increase the heat to high and cook, stirring constantly, for 2–3 minutes. Remove from the heat and drain in a sieve. Chop coarsely, season to taste and leave to cool.

2 Cut each sheet of pastry into six strips. Place a spoonful of spinach at the bottom of each strip. Scatter cheese and tomatoes on top. Fold the bottom right-hand corner of each strip up to meet the opposite side to form a triangle. Fold the triangle towards the top of the strip and repeat until you reach the top of the strip.

3 Brush the edges of each triangle with melted butter, then transfer to a greased baking tray. Brush the top of the parcel with more butter. Place the baking tray in the oven and bake for 10 minutes, or until the pastry is golden and crispy. Remove from the oven and serve at once. Alternatively, cool the triangles on a wire rack and serve warm or cold.

stuffed tomatoes

ingredients

MAKES 12

12 small ripe tomatoes about
    4.5-cm/1^3/$_4$-inches wide

1 large ripe avocado

1 tbsp lemon juice

4 tbsp mayonnaise

6 canned or bottled anchovy
    fillets in oil, drained and
    finely chopped

8 pitted black olives, finely
    chopped

pepper

snipped fresh chives,
    to garnish

method

1 Cut a thin slice from the base of each tomato and scoop out the seeds. Place cut-side down on several layers of kitchen paper and leave to drain.

2 Meanwhile, halve the avocado and remove the stone. Scoop the flesh into a bowl and mash with the lemon juice. Add the mayonnaise, anchovies and olives. Mix well and season with pepper to taste.

3 Spoon the avocado mixture neatly into the tomatoes. Arrange on a serving plate and sprinkle with snipped chives to garnish.

cheese puffs with fiery tomato salsa

ingredients

SERVES 8

70 g/2^1/$_2$ oz plain flour

50 ml/2 fl oz olive oil

150 ml/5 fl oz water

2 eggs, beaten

55 g/2 oz Manchego,
    Parmesan, Cheddar,
    Gouda or Gruyère cheese,
    finely grated

^{1}/$_2$ tsp paprika

vegetable or sunflower oil,
    for deep-frying

salt and pepper

fiery tomato salsa

2 tbsp olive oil

1 small onion, finely chopped

1 garlic clove, crushed

splash of dry white wine

400 g/14 oz canned chopped
    tomatoes

1 tbsp tomato purée

^{1}/$_4$–^{1}/$_2$ tsp dried red pepper
    flakes

dash of Tabasco sauce

pinch of sugar

salt and pepper

method

1 To make the salsa, heat the olive oil in a saucepan, add the onion and cook until softened but not browned. Add the garlic and cook for 30 seconds. Add the wine and let it bubble, then add the remaining salsa ingredients and simmer, uncovered, until a thick sauce is formed. Set aside. Meanwhile, prepare the cheese puffs. Sift the flour onto a plate. Put the olive oil and water in a pan and slowly bring to the boil. As soon as the water boils, remove the pan from the heat and quickly tip in the flour. Using a wooden spoon, beat the mixture well until it is smooth and leaves the sides of the pan.

2 Cool for 1–2 minutes, then gradually add the eggs, beating hard after each addition and keeping the mixture stiff. Add the cheese and paprika, season to taste with salt and pepper and mix well together. Heat the vegetable oil in a deep-fat fryer to 180–190°C/350–375°F. Drop teaspoonfuls of the prepared mixture, in batches, into the hot oil and deep-fry for 2–3 minutes, turning once, or until golden and crispy. They should rise to the surface of the oil and puff up. Drain well on kitchen paper. Serve the puffs piping hot, with the fiery salsa.

smoked salmon blinis

ingredients

SERVES 24

blinis

85 g/3 oz plain flour

1 tsp dried yeast

$^1/_2$ tsp sugar

150 ml/5 fl oz warm water

85 g/3 oz buckwheat flour

125 ml/4 fl oz warm milk

40 g/1$^1/_2$ oz butter, melted
    and cooled

1 large egg, separated

vegetable oil, for cooking

salt and pepper

topping

85 g/3 oz soured cream

finely grated rind of 2 lemons

55 g/2 oz smoked salmon,
    very finely sliced

pepper

2 tbsp very finely snipped
    chives, to garnish

method

1 To make the blinis, stir together the flour, yeast and sugar in a bowl. Make a well in the centre and slowly add the water, drawing in flour from the sides to make a wet, lumpy batter. Beat until the batter is smooth, then stir in the buckwheat flour, cover the bowl tightly with a tea towel and set aside for 1 hour until the batter has risen and the surface is covered with air bubbles.

2 Meanwhile, to make the topping, mix the soured cream with the lemon rind and pepper to taste. Cover and chill until ready to use. Stir the milk, butter and egg yolk together with a generous pinch of salt and pepper, then add to the batter, stirring well until blended. Beat the egg white in a separate bowl until peaks form, and then fold into the batter.

3 Heat a large frying pan over medium heat and lightly brush the surface all over with vegetable oil. Drop a tablespoon of the batter onto the hot surface so it forms a circle about 5 cm/2 inches across; add as many more as will fit in the pan without touching. Cook for just over a minute, or until the bottoms of the blinis are golden brown. Use a palette knife to flip them and cook on the other side until golden brown. Transfer to a heatproof plate and keep warm in a low oven while you cook the remaining batter.

4 To serve, arrange the warm blinis on a platter and top each with 2 teaspoons of the chilled soured cream. Lay the salmon strips over the soured cream, add the snipped chives and serve.

Club Mojito

ingredients

SERVES 1

1 tsp sugar syrup

few mint leaves

juice of $1/2$ lime

ice

2 measures dark rum

soda water

dash of Angostura bitters

mint leaves, to decorate

method

1 Put the syrup, mint leaves and lime juice into a glass and muddle.

2 Add the ice and rum and shake well. Pour into a glass and top up with soda water to taste.

3 Finish with a dash of Angostura bitters and decorate with mint leaves.

bellini

ingredients

SERVES 1

1 measure fresh peach
  juice made from lightly
  sweetened liquidised
  peaches
caster sugar
3 measures champagne,
  chilled

method

1 Dip the rim of a champagne flute into some peach juice and then into the sugar to create a sugar-frosted effect. Set aside to dry. Chill.

2 Pour the peach juice into the chilled flute and shake gently.

3 Top up with champagne.

cosmopolitan

ingredients

SERVES 1

2 measures vodka

1 measure Triple Sec

1 measure fresh lime juice

1 measure cranberry juice

ice

orange peel, to decorate

method

1 Shake all the liquid ingredients over ice until well frosted.

2 Strain into a chilled cocktail glass.

3 Dress with a strip of orange peel.

This edition published by Parragon Books Ltd in 2013

Parragon Books Ltd
Chartist House
15–17 Trim Street
Bath BA1 1HA, UK
www.parragon.com

ISBN: 978-1-4723-2693-5

Printed in China

Notes for the Reader
This book uses both metric and imperial measurements. Follow the same units of measurement throughout; do not mix metric and imperial. All spoon measurements are level: teaspoons are assumed to be 5 ml, and tablespoons are assumed to be 15 ml. Unless otherwise stated, milk is assumed to be full fat, eggs and individual vegetables are medium, and pepper is freshly ground black pepper. Unless otherwise stated, all root vegetables should be washed in plain water and peeled prior to using.

Garnishes, decorations and serving suggestions are all optional and not necessarily included in the recipe ingredients or method.

The times given are an approximate guide only. Preparation times differ according to the techniques used by different people and the cooking times may also vary from those given. Optional ingredients, variations or serving suggestions have not been included in the time calculations.

Recipes using raw or very lightly cooked eggs should be avoided by infants, the elderly, pregnant women, convalescents and anyone suffering from an illness. Pregnant and breastfeeding women are advised to avoid eating peanuts and peanut products. Sufferers from nut allergies should be aware that some of the ready-made ingredients used in the recipes in this book may contain nuts. Always check the packaging before use.